COC FOR BUSINESS

The Ingredients
For Sustainable Success

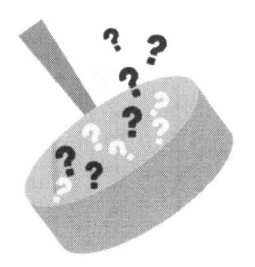

By
VANCE WITHERS

Copyright © Vance Withers 2019
This book is sold subject to the condition that it shall not, by way of trade or otherwise, be lent, resold, hired out, or otherwise circulated without the publisher's prior consent in any form of binding or cover other than that in which it is published and without a similar condition including this condition being imposed on the subsequent publisher.
The moral right of Vance Withers has been asserted.
© 496 Kitchen – part of the 496 Partnership
ISBN: 9781697157314

MAKING PEOPLE COUNT

DEDICATION

To my wife Karen and to my children Jamie, Elliot and Hannah for their love and always being there to support me.

CONTENTS

ACKNOWLEDGMENTS i
A NOTE FROM THE AUTHOR 1
WHAT'S THE BACKGROUND TO THE BOOK? 3
    What you'll learn 8
    What's the content based on? 12
    Where this book will help 14
IDENTIFYING THE INGREDIENTS FOR SUCCESS 17
    Can you have too many ingredients? 18
    Which ingredients are essential? 19
THE PROCESS 22
    How it works 23
    Utensils 31
    Seasoning 39
INGREDIENTS AND OUTLINES 50
    Building an Outstanding Team 55
    Making your company a great place to work 60
    The Awesome Appraisal 64
    Leading and Managing Change 68
    The Super Support Team 74
    The Great Leader 78
    The Exceptional Manager 82
    Running Effective Meetings 86
    The Super Salesperson 90

The Great Sales Call 95
  Making more of your time 99
  The Great Presenter 102
  The Win-Win Negotiation 106
MAKING THINGS HAPPEN 112
  Deciding on an action plan 112
SUMMARY 121
ABOUT THE AUTHOR.. 126

ACKNOWLEDGMENTS

To my first manager for supporting and believing in me and to the colleagues, clients and customers with whom I've shared so many learnings and wonderful adventures.

"Be courageous or be complacent.

Either way, you'll get the results that you deserve."

A note from the author

Thank you for your support in purchasing *Cooking for Business*. My key goal when writing the book was to produce a practical, no-waffle book that was easy to read and contained simple tools and tips. I wanted to combine my passions for developing people and cooking, to produce a book that was engaging and would provide a number of points of reference against which you could assess your business, your team or your processes. The lists of the 'key ingredients for success' are based on forty years of commercial experience and hundreds of workshops with directors and senior managers from all types of businesses in many different sectors. I've designed the book for you to be able to read in short bursts and apply the learnings or question yourself without the need to read the whole book in one go. I've tried to make it very practical in approach and content and I've been careful to outline precisely what steps need to be taken and how long they might take.

Like so many things in life, there are no guarantees of success, and I wanted you to be able to go as deep into the process as you want, relatively risk-free and without incurring further costs to you or to your business. To help you through the process, I've included a number of tools that over the years, I have found to be simple to understand and practical to use. Also, where appropriate, I've tried to use examples to help explain the process, the steps and the tools in a way that's easy to digest and therefore encourage you to go further.

My hope is that you will be able to quickly 'digest' the content whilst travelling or commuting and so use this 'down time' constructively and potentially uncover new ways of thinking about various aspects of your business.

I wish you good luck and every success however far you are able to take this process.

Best wishes,

Vance Withers

What's the background to the book?

I've been fortunate in my career to have worked with some very talented people, and have been supported and challenged by some great managers and mentors. Nothing has given me more satisfaction than being able to develop those people so that they could achieve their full potential – either in the roles that they were doing or by enabling them to secure well-deserved promotions. There's no greater feeling than seeing someone in whom you've invested time and who's responded well, doing great things and progressing with their own careers and lives. I've also experienced first-hand the effect that a supportive and knowledgeable manager and mentor can have on your personal development and professional outlook.

Alongside of my passion for developing people, I've also developed a passion for cooking, and I love nothing more than spending time in the kitchen, challenging myself to produce simple dishes well and to try new, potentially complicated recipes whenever I can. I love to cook from scratch and make things up as I go along but I know for new dishes or for consistent results, I need to follow a plan, a tried and tested plan – a recipe.

Strange as it might at first seem, I believe that the two disciplines (or passions) of cooking and developing people are very closely linked. Each one depends upon having the right ingredients, in the right amounts, mixing them carefully and allowing time for the flavours to bond together. Checking on progress regularly but not fussing – allowing time for the dish to cook correctly.

Achieving those things that you aspire to (such as a new meal or single dish) is much easier if you can follow a format that allows you to check that you've got the right things in place and you're doing the right things with them – a recipe in other words.

What if you could have a recipe book to guide you through commercial life? What if there was an easy to read, easy to understand reference document that allowed you to try new things, with the guidelines you needed to support you? Also, what if there was a list of ingredients that you could refer to help you structure your approach when trying to find new people, manage time better, have better meetings and so on?

My aim with this book was to provide a reference point to use either on its own or in conjunction with things that you're already doing. My aim was to challenge you to consider not only how you get the best 'ingredients' into your business but also to help you to understand how to treat them in the right way to get the best results.

The beauty about following a recipe is that not only will you have the right ingredients, but those ingredients will do the same for you as they've done for me and countless other managers and leaders. The challenge when dealing with individuals is that they all respond differently in different situations and often respond differently in the same situation. That's why it's difficult to guarantee results. It's also worth remembering that unlike cooking, if you ruin an 'ingredient' in commercial life, you can't simply get another one to replace it and start again. The beauty about dealing with people, however, is that even when you've made a mistake, you can recover the situation through dialogue and discussion.

You can use a recipe or any checklist to reassure yourself that you've got the right ingredients and that you're treating them in the right way. My goal was to produce was a book that could be a reference point that you could pick up and put down at any time to suit you. I certainly did not want you to have to read through everything and digest volumes of information. I've broken it into 'bite size' pieces to allow you to take things at your own pace.

As with most recipe books, you don't cook all the dishes at one time or indeed, if you ever will cook them all. They're a point of reference that are always to hand – where you need it and when you need it. It allows you to approach things 'just in time' rather than digest all the information 'just in case' you need it.

I also want you to be able to get straight to the detail – no waffle. I want you to have a 'recipe' against which you can check your resources and against which you can decide what's important for your business and what's critical if you are to achieve your mid- to long-term goals.

As I said previously, I've been fortunate to work with some great people and what I believe allowed those people to develop and grow is their ability to handle new ways of thinking and new ways of doing things. Their ability to review their ways of working and to challenge themselves to continually improve and never rest on their laurels. It's not that they try to change everything, far from it, but neither do they let things continue just because they've always been done in a certain way.

They act as the catalyst for change, for improvement and development. They bring others together, harness ideas and develop agreed actions. They support others in the pursuit of improvement.

> "If your actions inspire others to dream more, learn more, do more and become more, you are a leader."
> - John Quincy Adams

During my time working as a business trainer and consultant I found that it wasn't that people were anti-change or didn't seek personal improvement, it was just that they found it too difficult to get started. Breaking out of their day-to-day routines to try something different was often too big a step to take and spending days away from the office on a training course was something that just couldn't happen.

There are plenty of opportunities for 'down time' in anyone's working week, especially when using public transport. The space on a train or plane does not always create the best working space and using the laptop can certainly be challenging, but you can create your own self-contained environment in which to read something new.

Any new environment will create an opportunity for new ways of thinking. If you don't get the opportunity on public transport during your journey to work, take time out during the day to get up from your desk and move to a different space in the building. You will always get a fresh perspective on things.

What's important is that you try different and new approaches. Grabbing the opportunity for self-development is an extremely positive step to take. Working in isolation will prevent you having to feel awkward in front of other people. You can take things at your own pace and try things when you feel confident to do so. Also, to help get you started really quickly, I've included a number of tools (utensils) that I have found particularly useful during my time as a salesperson, manager, leader, coach and mentor. They're easy to understand and even easier to use.

Try them for yourselves – what downside could there possibly be?

If you try the new tools and don't feel comfortable with them or they don't give you the specific results that you're looking for, simply go back to the tools that you were using before. You've lost nothing but you will have gained a broader perspective.

WHAT YOU'LL LEARN

You'll know that with many things in life, different methods can produce the same results and that the same methods can result in different outcomes for different people. You'll also know that in cooking, different people cook the same meals using different ingredients. Cooking at a low temperature for a long time will give different results than cooking at a higher temperature for a shorter time. For example, you can't cook every joint of meat for the same time as they all vary in weight. Different ingredients deliver different results. Likewise, different people respond differently in similar situations – no two individuals can be treated identically. You have to remain flexible and adaptable.

Just having the right ingredients is not enough if you mistreat them and of course, no matter what you do with or to some ingredients, they can't become something else. Carefully boiling an egg won't turn it into a potato! Whilst on the subject of potatoes, that's one ingredient where treating it in a variety of ways will give you many different results.

I'd also like you to realise that even without all the ingredients, you can still make a great and delicious version of a dish – as long as you have the core ingredients in place.

What you'll find in each section is a list of potential ingredients, a list of what I believe are the essential ingredients and how to treat those ingredients to get the best results – consistently.

Use each section as a checklist before you start and as a guide as you progress. Share the contents with those you work with and use the content to challenge what you do as a business, as a team and as an individual. Invite input from those around you and use that input to tailor the content to suit your specific business needs.

Invest time to discuss the process and where it might lead you. Secure commitment and buy-in through those discussions but don't let that delay the process unduly. Be sure to document what you agree and monitor progress at regular intervals. Give feedback and recognise successes and individual achievements.

Use the book to stimulate your own thoughts and to provoke discussion. Reviewing the lists of ingredients will help you to realise exactly what you have at your disposal, what strengths you have and where you may need to increase knowledge or skills in order to be in a position to achieve the things that you want to. If you're approaching something for the first time and you don't know where to start, the individual recipes will help you to tackle new situations with confidence.

As a result of reading this book, I'd like you to think about different ingredients and think about treating them differently. I want you to understand the value of harnessing the energy of other people and working with them to develop robust action plans.

There are a number of 'ingredients' that need to be in place to get the best out this book and potentially, out of life itself. Without the following attributes or 'ingredients', you won't be able to fully realise your own or your organisation's potential.

Take time to reflect on yourself. Do you have the following 'ingredients' – these qualities and behavioural traits?

- Openness – do you have the ability or will to handle new information or thinking?
- Trust – do you have confidence in your people and your processes?

- Honesty – are you consistently 'telling it like it is'?
- Approachability – do you demonstrate your willingness to listen? Are you approachable?
- Humility – do you have the ability to admit when you've got it wrong?
- Tenacity – are you able to keep going when things get tough and keep trying until you get the results that you want?
- Resilience – can you handle setbacks? Do you learn from them and keep going?
- Dependability – can people count on you?

If you look at this list of 'ingredients' and can see yourself reflected, that's terrific. If not, then all is certainly not lost as these areas can be worked on as you progress on your own development journey.

If you're unsure, seek feedback from other people. Explain what you're trying to achieve and how their feedback will an invaluable part of the process. Ask for suggestions on how you might improve in certain areas and once you have that feedback, demonstrate that you have listened to the feedback and put whatever actions are appropriate in place to show that you can take feedback and will act upon it!

Once you have established your own performance, you can start to support those around you.

> "We look into mirrors but we only see the effects of our times on us – not our effects on others."
> - Pearl Bailey

WHAT'S THE CONTENT BASED ON?

The lists of ingredients are based on over forty years of discussions with individuals from over one hundred companies who were working at many different levels. I've been lucky enough to have facilitated countless discussions between directors and managers who have relished the chance to debate with their colleagues and to have input into what's needed to move their business forward listened to and recognised by their peer group. These discussions took place in a wide variety of businesses, operating in very different categories and markets. Input has been from individuals with varying levels of experience and knowledge but all with the same passion to make a difference.

The lists of ingredients are not exhaustive, but they are comprehensive. They're all statements relating to those actions and behaviours, the knowledge and the skills that the majority of Directors and

Managers saw as positive contributors in the quest to be the very best in each role or aspect of business described.

The reason that these discussions were always very energetic and productive is that people own what they help to create. If you've fought hard to secure a certain way of doing things or you've had your ideas incorporated into the ways in which your business operates, you are going to support those ideas and champion their implementation and development. You identify the key areas important to you and set resources and commitment to focus on them. It's well documented and proven that unless forced to do so by circumstances beyond your control, trying to change too many things at one time is a recipe for disaster.

Of course, you should know what needs to be changed and by how much it needs to change but that doesn't mean that you need to undertake all the changes at the same time. Allow yourself time to prioritise and set your objectives based on your ability and the ability of your organisation to handle the required changes balanced against the impact that those change will have on you, your business and your life. As part of the process, you should also take time to recognise what you're good at and celebrate that too. It's good to have something 'solid' and positive to hang onto in case things become challenging!

WHERE THIS BOOK WILL HELP

Although this process is extremely positive, it will be challenging at times. It's not going to create the impact you want without an agreed action plan to support and guide you through good times and tough times.

Of course, it's impossible to outline this plan as it will vary for everyone based on what you select as important and where you are performing against those criteria at the current time. You'll need to make sure you harness the energy from these sessions and use it to build a robust action plan that utilises the skill sets of everyone concerned. Use internal resources as well as external help. Use strong individuals to develop others. Use highly skilled individuals to train, mentor and develop others.

You will find that this process can bring different elements of your business together in ways you hadn't imagined. It will help different departments and teams to understand how others think – something which can bring long term benefits across the business.

Each chapter introduces a new subject and gives you the breakdown of the potential ingredients and unlike a list of ingredients for a specific dish, these recipes are designed to offer you a list of everything you could put into the mix. Like a recipe for a stew – you literally can put anything in that you like – it's all down to personal and family taste.

In our own cupboards or larders, we all keep a certain amount of ingredients on hand at all times. We even have ingredients that we have used only once but keep in the cupboard just in case! We will also buy in specific ingredients when they're essential for the dish in question.

So why is it when it come to our commercial worlds that we try to 'make do' with the ingredients that we have? Shouldn't we be 'buying in' the right ingredients to get the best results or at the very least, getting the very most out of those ingredients that we do have?

That sounds straightforward but one challenge that you'll face is that you don't have a recipe to follow. You have bits of recipes from previous roles and bits of recipes that people bring with them when they join your business. We make do and mend – often pulling together a real 'minestrone' of a dish – a combination of everything that we have to hand.

This book will help in a number of areas. It will challenge you to identify what you do have and what you may still require. It will help you to highlight the things that you do already and the things that you still need to do.

By following this approach, it will enable you to bring your team with you. Unlike cooking, running a business or working within a dynamic business are not solitary roles. You need the support of those around you. Securing a broad input will provide a solid platform from which to develop and grow into what you want to be or to develop a specific area of the business to be able to meet your future potential.

"No man will make a great leader who wants to do it all himself, or to get all the credit for doing it."
- Andrew Carnegie

Identifying the ingredients for success

For some people, having a vision of where they want to be or what they want to achieve is relatively straightforward. For example, in some industries and business sectors, the definition of success is simple and is defined by qualification or business capability. For most businesses and for most individuals, however, that definition of success is either harder to identify or even though we may know the results that we want to achieve, getting started on the process is difficult.

So, where do you start? What should you consider? Who should you involve? These are all frequently asked questions that can prevent an individual from getting started on new initiatives or tackling business or personal challenges.

As in cooking, there are a number of 'core' ingredients that are essential to be able to make or recreate a specific dish or meal. Once you have these, you can begin to incorporate other ingredients of your own choice.

You'll all be familiar with the saying "like Mama used to make" when referring to certain dishes. It's that aspect of personalisation that makes the recipes stand out from all the rest. That secret ingredient that one person includes that another doesn't. It's why the same dishes in different restaurants taste very different. Managing and controlling the ingredients and the processes at every stage and level is how certain restaurant and fast food chains can consistently replicate the same dishes and meals across different countries, with different people and with different suppliers.

CAN YOU HAVE TOO MANY INGREDIENTS?

The simple answer is "Yes."

When creating a dish or cooking a meal, there will come a point where you're unable to taste an ingredient as it's being overpowered by everything else. The same is true within your business. Trying to handle too many 'ingredients' will be a challenge – particularly if some are powerful enough to affect everything. Of course, the impact of too many spicy ingredients can be masked by simply layering in more and more neutral ingredients but what a waste of time and effort. Far better to identify the right level of 'spice' and manage the process from a 'constructive' point of view, rather than a 'corrective' point of view.

Also, if you haven't prepared a dish before, having a massive list of ingredients that need to be used can be daunting and often means that you just don't attempt the dish at all. The same is true in commercial life. If the number of things that you have to consider is too large, it's often easier to leave things as they are.

What's needed is a process where you can consider a wide number of options ('ingredients') but you also have the opportunity to 'filter' that list, to dismiss or remove ingredients that are 'nice to have' but not 'need to have'.

Certain ingredients will be critical and some will be essential when thinking about your own situation or that of your business. These are the ones that need to be acquired or developed if you are to achieve your desired results.

WHICH INGREDIENTS ARE ESSENTIAL?

This book is designed to give you the basic ingredients to deliver outstanding results in the following areas:

- Creating the most effective team
- Making your company a great place to work
- Conducting an awesome appraisal
- Leading and managing change
- Building a super support team
- Developing great leaders
- Creating exceptional managers
- Running effective meetings
- Creating the super salesperson
- Making each sales call great
- Making more of your time
- Becoming a great presenter
- Achieving Win-Win negotiations

In each section, you see a list of 'ingredients' written as a series of statements relating to certain knowledge and skills that may be required and certain behaviours that are critical. The 'mix' of ingredients required for success for you or your business is entirely down to you.

The lists are not exhaustive and there may be 'ingredients' that you want to include that aren't listed. If that happens, that's great. The purpose of the book is to provide guidelines and to provoke and facilitate discussions. I've always been a firm believer in the premise that people own what they help to create, so if there is a particular 'ingredient' missing, secure agreement from those directly concerned and simply add it to the final list.

However important this may be, you have to remember that it's not a race. Allowing time at the start of the process for people to have their input will pay back many times as you work through the process in your business.

The Process

Use the lists of ingredients as a reference and a checklist. Discuss the recipes with your colleagues and reach an agreement as to what goes in. Take time to identify those things which are critical and those things which are not listed but are important to you (based on culture, environment, industry, market etc.)

Set specific goals by department and with each key individual to ensure that your 'recipe' is delivered. Allow enough time for the 'flavours' to fully develop. Don't be impatient and expect results too quickly. Great results take time and are worth waiting for.

HOW IT WORKS

The process has four simple, straightforward steps:

STEP ONE – IDENTIFY AND AGREE

Nominate the key area(s) that you want to focus on. Secure agreement and commitment at this stage to ensure a smooth implementation or transition later.

STEP TWO – PLAN

Discuss, debate and agree what's critical and reduce the ingredients down to a manageable number.

STEP THREE – DO

Once agreed, identify what needs to happen to make these ingredients 'gel' together and build a solid action plan – with clear responsibilities and accountabilities.

STEP FOUR – REVIEW

Build in checkpoints to allow the process to flourish and grow. Set them at regular but infrequent intervals to avoid 'stifling' the process with too many interventions.

Please remember that whilst the process is straightforward, it will require commitment and consistent effort from everyone involved.

"Commitment is essential. Action is critical."

No amount of positive thinking will deliver results in isolation. There must be an agreed action plan in place. Not a complicated plan but a simple plan that everyone buys into and everyone knows exactly what's required and takes responsibility for delivering their part.

Let's look at each part of the process in more detail.

1 – Identify the key areas that you want to focus on

Based on the situation within your business, the results that you've achieved and the results that you're striving for, decide where you want to focus your efforts for maximum impact – both for short-term gain and for long-term sustainability. If required or if it's appropriate, gather your key stakeholders together and secure agreement on the areas on which you will focus.

Let's look at what might happen in a typical session. If we take the example of identifying the type of salesperson needed to deliver the future goals of the business, this becomes our 'frame of reference' and everything we discuss relates to it. With that in mind, we should quickly review all of the ingredients and start to note our preferred options. We should also be aware of anything specific that we believe is missing from the list and the members of the group should decide how to accurately describe that 'ingredient' in a clear, understandable and succinct way.

Once you're ready, set a time to meet with the stakeholders to start working through the process.

2 – Plan – Discuss, debate and agree what's critical

Discussion and debate are the key elements in ensuring that this process will be a success.

Bring all stakeholders together and confirm the objectives for the discussion. Split the group of stakeholders into two or three smaller groups and ask them to review the list of ingredients. Each of the smaller groups should work in isolation and use the time to reduce the overall number of ingredients down to a manageable level (fifteen ingredients max.). This can be done by simply reading the list of ingredients or you may find it has better impact and will promote better discussion if you make up separate cards with each of the individual ingredients on an individual card. These are simply laid out in front of the team and then each one is discussed, opinions are shared, the individual merits are discussed and agreement is reached as to whether it is desirable or essential for a successful outcome.

Work through the options and decide between the members of the group which ten to fifteen (max.) you are going to take back to the main group to debate and argue your case for inclusion in the final list.

If you have broken into three groups and each group identifies their top fifteen 'ingredients', don't expect that you will have agreement on every single item. Within organisations with clear values, goals and aspirations, there is good a chance that you'll get a high level of agreement across the groups. Based on my own experience, you should expect to get agreement on approximately one third of the 'ingredients'. You'll also find that even when there is a difference of opinion, the different groups have used one 'ingredient' to cover a number of different areas, rather than choosing all of them.

For example, it could be that one group has chosen a statement such as 'Is well organised' and another group doesn't have that specific 'ingredient' listed but does have a number of other – 'Manages time effectively', 'Sets priorities'. The first group may claim that they felt that their 'ingredient' covered the other group's choices and after some discussion, it could be that the other group agrees that one statement can cover a number of areas. As long as everyone understands what each of the 'ingredients' actually means and requires of the organisation, then reducing the number or inserting another 'priority' is a great option.

Do not try to rush this stage of the process. There is no time limit and it's certainly not a race. This will be one of the first occasions that a broad cross section of your team has been able to sit together to openly discuss key aspects of your business. To be able to have an input into what will or might happen is incredibly motivating for all participants and time should be allowed for open discussion, questioning and ultimately, agreement.

3 – Do – Identify the essential actions

Once you've decided on your list of the top ten or top twelve 'ingredients', you'll need to consider how you go about delivering this to the business. You chose the area that you wanted to work on and you have now chosen the key ingredients that you need to have in place in order to 'make' your end goal – to deliver what you see as 'best in class' for your business and your team.

In describing your 'best in class' list of ingredients, it's very unlikely that you don't have some of these in place at the moment. They may not be performing at the level you need or delivering what you want, but they are in place.

Take time to rank your business, your team or individuals within the team against the list of ingredients that you have identified – a mark of '10' would denote that there's no work to do and everything is as it should be. A mark of '1' would indicate that there is a great deal of work to do. Once this assessment is complete, you can begin to identify and agree the actions needed to get you from where you are to where you want to be

For example, if you look at the area of appraisals overall, if you have an appraisal process in place and it's delivering what you want, you'd score it a '10' overall. If you don't have an appraisal system in place it would definitely score a '1' and if you if you have an appraisal process in place but it's lacking in overall effectiveness and not delivering what you want, it's likely to get an assessment of '3' to '4'.

If you have a process in place but it's not consistently used or people just aren't giving it the right focus, your list of ingredients will give you clear targets to aim for and each one will need focus and effort.

You'll be able to take the right ingredients and use the right 'utensils' with the right amount of 'seasoning' to deliver the results that you want.

Plan to take your time and certainly do not try to rush things. Manage people's expectations – make it clear what's acceptable and what is not acceptable. You should absolutely get on with things as soon as you possibly can, but you should not expect results to come immediately. You may get some quick wins and because they helped to create it, people are more likely to give the new way of working much more attention.

4 – Review – Build in checkpoints

As I've written earlier, the similarities between cooking and business or people development are what prompted me to write the book. Each of them depends upon having the right ingredients, in the right amounts, mixing them carefully and allowing time for the flavours to bond together. Checking on progress regularly but not fussing – allowing time for the dish to cook correctly.

Watch any of the great chefs and they don't fuss over their cooking. They use the best of ingredients, treat them in a way that experience has told them will get the best results and then allow enough time to ensure that they completely fuse together. They check at regular intervals, but they certainly aren't constantly lifting the saucepan lid to see what's going on and they certainly do not consistently fuss over the dish or prod and poke it to somehow hurry things along.

Take a typical spicy dish like a chilli. As with many other spicy dishes, you get the best results if you make it and leave it for a while before serving, thereby allowing the flavours to intensify. Rushing them only produces a 'lightweight' version of this classic dish. Sure, it's edible, but imagine how great it could have been!

So, set the process in motion and agree the action plan. Let things develop at the pace that you've all agreed. Set specific milestones and review dates and keep to them. Make the reviews too often and you look like you're 'fussing' over things and you won't necessarily get the best out of your people. On the other hand, if you allow too much time between reviews, you run the risk of the process becoming stalled or 'bogged down' and potentially people could lose interest. It's like the difference between using too much heat too quickly, or not using enough heat, which affects the overall cooking time. Either way, the dish could be ruined.

You should allow yourself time to review and therefore time to celebrate if things go well and to take corrective action if they don't. If things are going well, it gives you the opportunity to drive things at a faster pace. If things are not going well, it allows you to see this very quickly and to take action to get the process back on track.

This is precisely why you don't take on too many things at once. If you spread yourself too thinly, you run the risk of not being able to control the process. Far better to attempt less and be able to focus. You'll probably find that in focusing on fewer things, you get stuff done quicker, the results come much quicker and you can then move onto another area. Success will breed success and that momentum that you develop will become a very potent and powerful force.

> "It takes as much energy to wish as it does to plan."
> - Eleanor Roosevelt

UTENSILS

For those of you who love to know these things, the word *utensil* comes from the Latin **utensilia** meaning 'things for use'.

The definition of a utensil in respect of the cooking process or kitchen environment is an item that is used to aid the cooking process or to complete the eating process. Likewise, in this book, the utensils will be those items that you use to drive, support, monitor, review, realign, adjust and control the process. These 'utensils' are vital at the start of the process and should be used at regular intervals to maintain momentum and commitment. I've included examples for you reference later in the book. The 'utensils' or items in question are:

1. Meeting environment
2. Vison of success (pictures)
3. Objective sheet

4. Feedback process
5. Project planner
6. Performance Improvement Grid

Of course, you may already have suitable tools ('utensils') established within your business. Using these will enable participation at a quicker pace and with more broad commitment. If you don't have the tools in place, then use the templates and tailor them to your own business environments and cultures. Be careful not to spend too long deciding on the format and structure of tools as this will impact on your ability to get started and delivering results as quickly as you'd hoped for.

Meeting Environment

Be sure to choose a 'neutral' office or meeting space to kick off the process. This 'new' space will be critical in encouraging people to see things in a different way and will promote creative thinking. Make sure that you are not 'shackled' by keeping to the same protocols as you use in daily business. New environments allow new thinking – it's as simple as that.

Also, it's good practice in a meeting such as this to ensure all mobile phones are switched off or better still, don't allow them in the room!

Vision of Success

Consider building or collecting a library of pictures that help you to express what you're trying to create. It's often easier to describe what you mean by using a picture, rather than attempting to explain precisely what you mean just by using words. You may have your own images that you want to use, or you can easily download 'stock' pictures. You could even simply cut out from a selection of magazines. It's entirely your choice!

Images allow for total clarity and avoid misinterpretation.

One example of this 'visioning' approach, is the Mood Board which agencies will use to convey how a product or brand should feel to the consumer. Interior designers also use this approach as it enables many ideas to be tied together in a way that everyone can see the 'big picture'.

Objective/Goal Sheet

Commit those things that have been agreed to writing.

Set review dates and stick to them.

Be very specific in what you describe – be S.M.A.R.T.

Specific – what precisely are you trying to achieve?

Measurable – can you measure it? How will you measure it?

Agreed – does everyone sign up for what's required?

Realistic – is it actually 'do-able'?

Timed – over what time period have you set the challenge?

A simple example of an Objective or GOAL sheet:

Current Situation	Objective	Key Actions	Status

One way to keep track of progress so that everyone can see exactly what's going on at any time, is to use a traffic light system in the 'status' box:

Green = achieved / Orange = in progress / Red = not started

Feedback process

Agree the procedure for feedback and progress monitoring right up front and develop standard formats to allow easier sharing of information.

One useful tool is the **GROW** model which you can find in a multitude of different formats – my preference is:

Goal – what were we trying to achieve?

Reality – where are we/what progress have we made?

Options – what should we/could we be considering?

What Next – next steps and key actions

Feedback should be ongoing – regular but not so frequent as to stifle the process. Some things will take time and it's pointless coming back to the group to report 'no progress'. So, keep feedback timely and honest; make sure that you act on what the feedback is telling you. If it looks like things are going off track, act to change things. Far better to make more regular, smaller adjustments than ignore things for too long and have to make a much larger adjustment sometime in the future.

Always remember that people own what they help to create so get input whenever and wherever you can.

Tell people what's happening – even if it's not good news or you haven't made the progress you were hoping for. Staying silent will appear as if you're hiding something and once doubt creeps into the process, any future progress will be slow and could even stop as people become disillusioned and disappointed.

Project planning sheet

If you're undertaking a far-reaching or radical programme of change, it's critical that you brainstorm all required actions/steps before agreeing to a specific action plan.

There will be a natural and logical order in which things should happen and it's useful to follow that logic to keep everything simple and straightforward.

Make sure that you agree responsibilities for all key tasks and be certain to circulate to all stakeholders.

There are many useful formats to use. My favourite is the GANTT chart, named after its inventor, Henry Gantt, who designed the format around 1910. Today, there are many software solutions that you can get 'off the shelf' to help you produce such a document but at its heart, it's a very simple concept (see the following example).

You detail the key actions down the left-hand side of the chart and the time frame is depicted along the top of the sheet. You can then use a simple method of coloured blocks to indicate when the actions need to be completed in order to complete the overall objective in the required time.

You can use different coloured blocks to indicate different responsibilities or you can write people's names into the blocks. It's entirely up to you. The key thing is to have some sort of control document in place right from the very start. Once you've got things underway, it will be very difficult to complete a GANTT chart retrospectively.

Example GANTT Chart

Sales Development Programme		Week												
Key Action	Responsibility	1	2	3	4	5	6	7	8	9	10	11	12	13
Confirm launch of new initiative	DP	■												
Notify trade press	AF	■	■											
Agree product support programme	BC		■	■										
Brief internal operations teams	DP		■	■										
Brief sales teams	RM			■										
Brief key customers	RM			■	■									
Brief tender for training programme	RM				■	■								
Confirm training partner	DP					■	■							
Complete fieldwork and analysis	FG						■	■						
Write programme	FG							■	■					
Run initial training session	RM									■				
Review and follow up	RM											■	■	
1st Phase formal review	RM & DP													■

Performance Improvement Grid – P.I.G.

I go into this in more detail later in the book but it's absolutely my most favourite tool because of its simplicity and ease of use.

It allows you to be really specific about pretty much anything, in any situation. It can be used at the start of the process to identify key actions or it can be used part way through the initiative to monitor progress and reset the path.

Whatever question you ask, the four quadrants will give you the answers you need to get started, get back on track, give recognition, give a gentle nudge – really, whatever you need it to do!

So, whether the question is "what do we need to do?" or "what progress have we made?" you ask the same questions:

What is it that we will **Start Doing**?

What is it that we will **Stop Doing**?

What do we need to **Do Differently**?

In what areas do we need to **Do More**?

The key to success is always preparation. Investing time at the front end will always pay dividends later on.

> "Give me six hours to chop down a tree and I will spend the first four sharpening the axe."
> - Abraham Lincoln

SEASONING

In cooking, the substances added to other foods to enhance their flavour and smell and overall palatability are referred to as seasoning. We would often think of salt and pepper as good, safe, go-to seasonings but there are many others such as herbs, spices, oils, and vinegars. However, it is generally agreed that any substance that can be added to a recipe to provide the desired flavour, such as sweet, spicy, intensely hot, sour, tangy, or earthy, is added as a seasoning.

In the context of this book and this process, I want to take you through what I think are the main 'seasonings' that you need to build into the process in order to significantly and positively affect the end result. Of course, how much you 'add' is up to you and in some cases, the process just won't work without them. As in cooking, some of the seasonings can be added only once, others need to be added throughout the cooking process as the flavour develop. The same is true with the following areas that I want you to think about:

- Feedback
- Recognition
- Reward

Too much of any one of these can make the whole process a little too 'sweet'. Too little of any of these can make the process a little bit 'sour'.

Let's look at them in more detail.

Feedback

Feedback should be:

- Timely

    You should plan that if you see something, either positive or negative, you give feedback as close as possible to the time that you made your observations. You may choose to delay feedback to ascertain if it was an isolated occurrence but make sure you make detailed notes so that you can accurately recall what happened.

- **Honest**

    You should agree to 'tell it as it is'. Be sensitive but don't dress things up and don't soften things too much.

- **Fair**

    Take account of the situation or environment in which you made your observations and deliver the feedback in a way or in a place that respects the individual or teams concerned.

- **Objective**

    Facts are critical. Avoid opinions. Don't try to interpret and second guess.

- **Balanced**

    Look for the good as well as the not so good. It's unlikely that the feedback to be delivered will be all negative so make sure that you give praise as well as point out where improvements could be made.

- **Open**

    Avoid creating 'off limits' subjects or areas. Agree up front the breadth and depth of feedback that will be required.

Remember, too much feedback overall or over-positive feedback could 'overcook' things or make them too 'sweet'. Too little feedback or too much critical feedback will cause 'bitterness' and the end result could be undercooked!

> "We all need people who will give us feedback. That's how we improve."
> - Bill Gates

Recognition

It's important to agree the process and frequency to give recognition. You need to get the balance right. For some people, a simple 'thank you' for a job well done is all that they need. For others, being praised in public or seeing their name in lights is what's required. Whatever approach you take, be sure to make the recognition of effort and results achieved a key part of your plans.

- **Public recognition**

    Widely circulated emails are a great way to deliver recognition for a job well done. Of course, not everyone likes to be in the spotlight, but it will create a sense of progress and achievement.

- **Private**

    There will be times when a quick word in private to an individual will be enough to say that you've recognised their efforts and achievements.

- **Internal**

    Newsletters, bulletin boards, notice boards – use whatever 'tools' you have to keep the message front of mind.

- **External**

    Trade publications are a great way of signalling to your customers the efforts that you're going to make their experiences in dealing with you even better. Be careful not to give too many secrets away, but don't do loads of great work and not tell anyone!

- **Verbal**

    A simple 'thank you' is often all that's needed to make someone 'feel like a million dollars'.

- **Written**

    A personal note – particularly from a senior member of the team – will always be positively received. It takes minimal time to write it.

Reward

There's always an element of any change process where the question of "what's in it for me?" comes up. Now, I'm not advocating that you start a whole new incentive or remuneration programme but would encourage you to think about ways you can reward individual or team efforts in a reasonable, cost-effective way.

A simple night out or a celebration meal is sufficient enough. Getting people together to celebrate milestones is really motivating. You could consider individual rewards, but it's far more effective in broad-based initiatives to focus on rewarding the team as a whole.

Agree what results are required (milestones) and then agree what will happen once they have been achieved or surpassed.

> "People work for money but go the extra mile for recognition, praise and rewards."
> - Dale Carnegie

Getting Started

So, you've chosen the area that you want to look at and you've notified the team to set the meeting date and venue. Let's look again at what the next steps are and how we get things started.

Once you've committed to try this process, agreed dates and you've managed to get the group together, take the group through how things will work and explain the process as follows:

Start by outlining the area that you'll be focusing on and explain the reasons behind your choice. It's important to set the scene and secure buy-in right at the start. It's also important to confirm that everyone should participate fully and should feel free to express their views openly and honestly. Please expect that some individuals may find this difficult to start with but be confident that once the process begins, they'll find it difficult not to contribute!

Confirm to the group that they'll be working in two, three or maybe four smaller groups. They'll be working together to discuss all the 'ingredients' and their objective is to decide within their group what the most important ten to twelve items are. Of course, it's entirely up to you to set the number of how many options they should bring back to the table, but you'll find that it's better to agree a smaller number as choosing too many options could slow the overall process down. You should allow 45-60 minutes (maximum) to complete this stage. It's important to keep an eye across each of the groups to see what progress is being made and, if they finish the task quicker, there's no harm in regrouping ahead of schedule. However, do ensure that they take the opportunity to debate each ingredient fully.

Once each group has the required number of 'ingredients', you should bring all the groups back together and ask them to be ready to share their choices, their reasons for those choices and to debate with the other groups, if necessary, to secure selection of a particular 'ingredient' if they feel strongly that it should be part of the final list.

This stage is about debating the various pros and cons of any suggestion and ending up with a selection of 'ingredients' that they *all* agree on.

Agree the criteria for selection into the final list based on the number of smaller groups that you have. For example, if you have three groups debating with each other the rules for selection could be as follows:

If all three groups have selected an 'ingredient' for inclusion, it automatically makes the final list.

If two out of the three groups have selected an option, you should put it on a reserve list and take a view for inclusion based on the number of 'ingredients' that all groups agree on. So, if all three groups agree on all ten to twelve options, there is no need for this reserve list.

If only one of the groups selects a particular 'ingredient', they should share their rationale for choosing that particular one and challenge the group to secure inclusion on the reserve list if they feel strongly enough about it.

Clearly, if none of the groups select a particular 'ingredient', then it definitely won't make the final list.

It could also be that the groups bring one of their own 'ingredients' to the table – something that they didn't feel was covered by any other option. In this instance they should present their new suggestion, explain the rationale and debate with the other groups to establish the merits (or otherwise) of their choice.

Eventually through a process of debate and elimination, you will arrive at your final number of 'ingredients' that everybody agrees on. At this point it's probably a good idea to take a well-earned break!

Once you have the final list, you should circulate it to all participants and give everyone involved time to reflect and to become comfortable with it. Of course, you could carry straight on from your earlier session, but you'll find that the process will work much better if you give people time (but only a short time) to review the agreed choices in private.

Once the dust has settled and people have had time to reflect, it's time to move onto the next phase.

How much time will I need?

With today's increasingly busy schedules and with multiple commitments, it's critical to understand how much time you should allow before you start out on the process.

Depending on your specific business requirements, simply identifying the area on which to focus can take time but it's critical that you secure commitment across the all departments right at the start.

Once you've agreed which area you're going to focus on, the following timings are typical of what you can expect for the first sessions in order to gain the most value for you, your team and your business.

The time required for subsequent actions, follow up and review will clearly depend upon the scale of the project that you undertake.

1 – Assemble and brief stakeholders

30-45 mins

Set the scene, explain the process and agree expectations.

2 – Split into groups and discuss

60-90 mins

Discuss all potential ingredients until a decision is made on the priority selection.

3 – Review conclusion together

60-90 mins

Review each ingredient and establish common agreement to enable reduction to the final list.

4 – Agree priority actions

90-120 mins

Agree actions and set review dates. Agree specific responsibilities for each area.

Let's get started!

"Never give up on a dream just because of the time it will take to accomplish it. The time will pass anyway."
- Earl Nightingale

Ingredients and Outlines

The following pages contain list of potential ingredients for you to consider, discuss and if necessary, add something specific that's needed within your business or business sector.

The lists cover the following areas:

- Creating the most effective team
- Making your company a great place to work
- Conducting an awesome appraisal
- Leading and managing change
- Building a super support team

- Developing great leaders
- Creating exceptional managers
- Running effective meetings
- Creating the super salesperson
- Making each sales call great
- Making more of your time
- Becoming a great presenter
- Achieving Win-Win negotiations

Before each list of ingredients, I've provided a brief outline of what you need to be thinking about and where appropriate, I've also included a tool to help the process – either at this early stage or during the period of implementation.

It's doubtful that you'll find you have none of the ingredients available. It's far more likely that already you have a great deal of them in place but over time you've come to take them for granted. If nothing else, this book will remind you of what you did to get you where you are, where you need to refocus and what you need to put in place.

This is completely natural and all of us go through the same process whatever we're involved in. It's called The Learning Cycle and it looks like this:

Unconscious Incompetence
You don't think about what you don't know

Unconscious Competence
You don't think about what you know

Conscious Incompetence
You think about what you don't know

Conscious Competence
You think about what you know

Before we start on any new initiative or whenever we take up a new sport or get involved in a new hobby, we are not aware of what we don't know or can't do because we have never had occasion to think about it.

When we do start to look in more detail, we suddenly become aware of what's involved and we also become aware of the fact that we're not very good at doing what we're supposed to do. Think about the first time you rode a bike or drove a car. You suddenly realise how difficult it seems. You want to do it, but you know that you can't.

As you get more into whatever it is that you're doing for the first time, you'll get to the point where everything clicks into place. You can suddenly balance on the bike, you can strike the golf ball very sweetly or you can drive without crashing the gears! Now, although you can do it, you are aware of everything that you're doing. You're consciously going through the process as you do it.

Because you've been getting better at your new pastime, you're growing in confidence. In fact, you can do what you need to do without thinking about it. You've become 'Unconsciously Competent' and you really start to enjoy yourself.

Now, life would be great if we achieved this level of competence and we maintained it. For most of us however, once we've crossed those early milestones, we start to acquire bad habits and our effectiveness, or our skill levels and/or knowledge levels start to decline. Without realising it, we've drifted back into 'Unconscious Incompetence'. We're not actually as good as we thought we were.

In most sports and in many businesses, the top performers have a coach or mentor who works with them to make sure that they stay at the top of their game. Through assessment, feedback and practice, they're able to consistently play their best shots or make the best decisions and if their performance levels start to tail off, they work together to build an action plan to get back to the level that they need to be.

That's what this book is all about. I want you to find time to reflect on your current performance, understand what's happening, why it's happening and put an action plan in place to get back to where you need to be or to start out on a new path to even greater success.

Even the most experienced cooks will follow a recipe when doing something for the first time and will certainly review their processes if a dish goes wrong or doesn't come out as planned.

> "For good ideas and true innovation, you need human interaction, conflict, argument and debate."
> - Margaret Heffernan

Remember, this is not a quick process and whilst you could be tempted to try and shortcut the process, to get the best results you need to follow the 'recipe' and allow the right amount of time. The time needed will vary depending upon the focus area itself, the number of people that are involved and the strength of feelings amongst the participants. To get to an action plan that everyone agrees with will take time but the end results are worth waiting for.

As with cooking in general, getting the right ingredients in place is just the start but follow the process, the 'recipe', and those ingredients are transformed into a fabulous end product.

The 'recipe' summary:

1 – Outline the focus area

30-45 mins

2 – Split into groups and debate

60-90 mins

3 – Debate conclusions and agree final list

60-90 mins

4 – Agree priority actions and responsibilities

90-120 mins

BUILDING AN OUTSTANDING TEAM

When we think of successful and effective teams, we often think of the sporting arena, where there are many examples of truly great teams. However, effective teams can be found in all aspects of life – sports and commercial. Individuals from different backgrounds, with different educations and different experiences and skills, all working together to achieve a common goal is something that you see in all walks of life.

But, what can we learn from these most successful teams? What is it that they do to make themselves successful and how do we replicate those things? There is no one simple answer but there are number of things that all teams do that we can learn from and imitate for your own teams and businesses.

Take my favourite team example – a Formula 1 Pit Crew. They make changing four wheels in three seconds look easy but is it really that simple? How do you think they got to be so good at the task? Firstly, they all have clear roles and clear responsibilities – they are accountable for what they do. They all understand the impact doing or not doing their task will have on the other members of the team and on the achievement of the overall goal. They work hard at being a team. They practice over and over again, not until they can get it right but until they can't get it wrong.

Most importantly of all I believe is that they trust each other to do what they have to do. So, even though they may think that they're all finished and their hands are in the air to signal that all is good to go, if the man on the paddle board at the front doesn't release the car then nothing happens. Even though it may seem like an eternity at times, they all trust that man to know when it's safe for the driver to leave the pit lane. For that time when the car is in the pit, the most highly paid of all of the team, is not in control. The man with the paddle board has control for that brief time in the pits and they all respect that.

That's how it works – time and time again.

I'm sure that most of you will be familiar with the four stages of building a successful team:

Forming - bringing the members of the team together.

Storming - where each member tests every other to find the limits and tolerances.

Norming - where people learn to work together, to recognise each other's contribution.

Performing - effectively working together to achieve goals.

This is the natural process that occurs and we all have to go through each stage when we are trying to build a truly effective team. However, how long you stay in each stage can be influenced by the amount of effort that you're prepared to put in and the level and openness of communication that you establish.

Using this approach will enable you to establish common ground right at the start, thereby reducing the time that you spend 'Storming' and allowing you to move into 'Norming' and 'Performing' in the shortest period of time.

> "Coming together is a beginning, staying together is progress and working together is success."
> - Henry Ford

Ingredients to build an outstanding team:

- Share objectives with each other
- Have clear roles, responsibilities and accountabilities
- Trust each other
- Create an environment where people help each other
- Make time for each other
- Stand up for and support each other
- Work together to solve problems
- Communicate effectively with each other
- Believe in your goals and objectives
- Regularly challenge each other
- Have clear expectations of each other
- Listen to each other
- Believe in each other
- Create a culture where people care about the business
- Regularly review our performance
- Celebrate success
- Deal with any problems effectively
- Encourage each other
- Regularly try different ways to do things
- Be open to change
- Team members are willing to go the extra mile
- Build a non-political culture
- Work to a set of agreed 'ground rules'
- Link appraisals to your personal development plans
- Ensure that everyone is open to feedback
- Use team/individual strengths to develop others

- Have clearly defined values
- Uphold your values in everything you do
- Explain what people can do to make a difference
- Treat individuals fairly
- Treat each other with respect
- Maintain a flexible approach
- Encourage new ideas
- Make time for personal development
- Have a common view of what good looks like
- Ensure team members know how to motivate each other
- Maintain a low staff turnover
- Make sure that team members are engaged at all times
- Don't ever rest on your laurels
- Admit your mistakes quickly and take corrective action
- Recognise individual and team success
- Share learnings with each other
- Have a clear team identity
- Encourage prudent risk-taking
- Work well with other teams
- Recognise individual contributions
- Build success
- Work hard
- Have an active social network
- Get things done
- Work effectively together
- Harness each other's strengths to achieve results
- Share objectives with other departments
- Have fun together

- Take time to understand what motivates each other
- Always try to do the right thing
- Strive to make decisions that benefit the whole team
- Make decisions quickly
- Do what it takes to get the job done
- Tell it as it is
- Be prepared to listen to each other
- Be proud of each other

MAKING YOUR COMPANY A GREAT PLACE TO WORK

For many people, the desire to work for a great company is overwhelming. The need or desire to be part of a fast-moving, positive, productive, rewarding and empowering culture is truly motivating. On the flip side, however, the fact that you see your business as failing in key areas can also be demotivating and frustrating. So, what can you do about it?

You can simply muddle on and accept what you have, or you can work with those around you, identify what you want to achieve with your business and the way it operates and take the appropriate actions to deliver desired outcomes.

Complacency is the enemy of progress and whilst you want your people to be comfortable at work and happy in what they do, you should not let that become a barrier to progress. Let it become a safeguard to make sure that whatever changes you might make, they only enhance the experience of working for your business. They don't detract from it.

Set out what you want to be – the biggest, the most profitable, the preferred supplier in your area – and work out that means in real terms. Set the hard goals (the 'what') and use the list of ingredients to identify your 'how' goals. What do you need to do to deliver on your aspirations of making yours a great company to work with and to work within?

> "An organisation's ability to learn and to translate that learning into action rapidly, is the ultimate competitive advantage."
> - Jack Welch

Ingredients for making your company a great place to work:

- Have a clear company goal
- Have defined roles, responsibilities and accountabilities
- Understand your customers
- Create an environment where people help each other
- Support childcare/crèche facilities
- Be profitable
- Invest in your people
- Invest in your systems
- Reward employees fairly
- Ensure everyone has an up-to-date Personal Development Plan
- Make appraisals and performance management a way of life
- Have a clear long-term plan for the business
- Have a defined succession plan
- Control expenses
- Create a culture where people care about the business
- Share the success of the business amongst the employees
- Celebrate success
- Make it is easy for your customers to do business with you
- Ensure that your customers know what you stand for
- Invest in product/service development
- Have clearly defined career paths
- Talk to each other effectively
- Be a non-political organisation

COOKING FOR BUSINESS

- The senior team understand what happens at ground level
- Customers enjoy trading with us
- Be the company of choice for all stakeholders
- Have fun
- Have clearly defined values
- Uphold your values in everything that you do
- Make sure people know what is expected of them
- Ensure that managers invest time in their people
- Promote from within where possible
- Be flexible
- Embrace change
- Know what your customers think of you
- Have an effective, simple and robust planning system
- Keep your people motivated
- Maintain a low staff turnover
- Actively manage talent in the organisation
- Have great leaders in all key positions
- Proactively monitor employee engagement
- Ensure everyone has clear picture of what success looks like
- Have a clear company mission
- Encourage prudent risk-taking
- Build a reputation for treating people fairly
- Ensure senior managers communicate directly with their teams
- Facilitate flexible working
- Work hard and play hard
- Have an active social network
- Have an established programme of job sharing/swapping
- Have meetings only if you have something to say

- Ensure senior managers meet regularly with all employees
- Build a comprehensive recognition programme
- Allocated budgets for training your people
- Know what your competitors do well
- Know what we have to do to improve in key areas
- Have assigned teams to manage our key customers
- Hold regular top-to-top meetings with key partners
- Have a system for dealing with underperformance
- Install high standards of performance across the business
- Be open with each other and tell it as it is
- Demonstrate that every employee makes a difference

THE AWESOME APPRAISAL

It never ceases to amaze me how something so positive as an appraisal process can become a chore for some businesses and can be often used as a 'weapon' against people rather than a tool to support, encourage and develop the talent within a business.

There is a weight of opinion at the moment that recommends getting rid of the annual appraisal process all together and replacing it with monthly or quarterly reviews as this will save time, money and be less stressful for the employees. In my opinion, they clearly have had a very negative experience of the whole appraisal process, a process which is often seen as an administrative chore rather than a motivational exercise. The truth is that no one does a perfect job and not many people consistently do a great job. Everyone has strengths and everyone has development areas. Weak managers who don't want to have challenging conversations either just focus on the positives or worse still, ignore the appraisal process all together.

There should not be any surprises at an annual appraisal meeting. Individuals should be aware of how they're doing before they enter the room. The appraisal meeting is about looking forward as much (if not more) than looking back.

Give plenty of notice to make sure that the participants have time to fully prepare. They should not and must not feel like they are being pressured into something over which they have no control.

Make sure that you invite feedback about yourself and listen to what's being said to you. Avoid being defensive and be prepared to act on the feedback that you receive.

Make sure that you set realistic goals, both commercial and personal goals and discuss how you can work together to achieve what you both want to achieve.

As well as giving the other person time to prepare, holding the appraisal in a neutral, private room will ensure that discussions can be open, honest and relaxed. I've seen appraisals taking place in hotel foyers, on trains and even on board an aeroplane. Needless to say, the discussions were not exactly open and were certainly very one sided.

Having an appraisal system in place is a great start but do make sure that it's fit for purpose today. Things change very quickly and you need to make certain that the process and the tools allow you to achieve what you want to achieve.

It can be a very positive and rewarding way of spending one to two hours with your employees – as long as it's without interruption. Give the process and the meetings the time that they deserve and enjoy the results!

> "You've got to be rigorous in your appraisal system. The biggest cowards are managers who don't let people know where they stand."
> - Jack Welch

Ingredients for an awesome appraisal:

- Both parties are fully prepared
- Annual discussions are supported with quarterly reviews
- Meeting dates are agreed in advance
- What's being appraised is clear and agreed
- Feedback is honest
- Feedback is two-way
- Contains relevant, up-to-date examples
- Is objective
- Is non-judgemental
- Demonstrates flexibility
- Demonstrates empathy
- Contains genuine praise
- Sets realistic goals
- Has an agreed action plan
- Links to a broader personal development plan
- Is held in a suitable venue
- Is not rushed
- Is based on facts, not opinions
- Allows for open discussion
- Builds on strengths as well as identifying weaknesses
- Is motivational
- Is seen as a good use of time
- Is consistent across the business
- Assess and measures common criteria
- Is documented
- Is agreed by both parties
- Is not linked to salary discussions

- Focuses on the 'why' as well as the 'what'
- Does not take too long
- Follows an agreed format

LEADING AND MANAGING CHANGE

The only constant that we face is change and rest assured, the pace of that change will get even quicker. Today's new invention is tomorrow's retro or vintage item. Obsolescence can happen overnight.

As a business or as an individual, our ability to recognise the need for change, embrace it and feel comfortable in the process is of paramount importance. The days of working with a system or with a specific tool for year upon year are way behind us and our ability to embrace and adapt will define our opportunity for success. Successfully leading or managing change requires a simple and logical set of controls to be in place.

Start with 'Why'

The natural reaction to any change initiative is fear. People get worried by what they don't understand. It's critical to make sure that everyone concerned with the change knows why things are changing. They need to understand what specifically needs to change, how much it needs to change by to be deemed a success and what they specifically need to do to help manage and drive the change through the business.

There five critical components to any change process and without any one of these in place, the change initiative will stall or certainly the pace will slow down. It could even lead to a complete failure of the process.

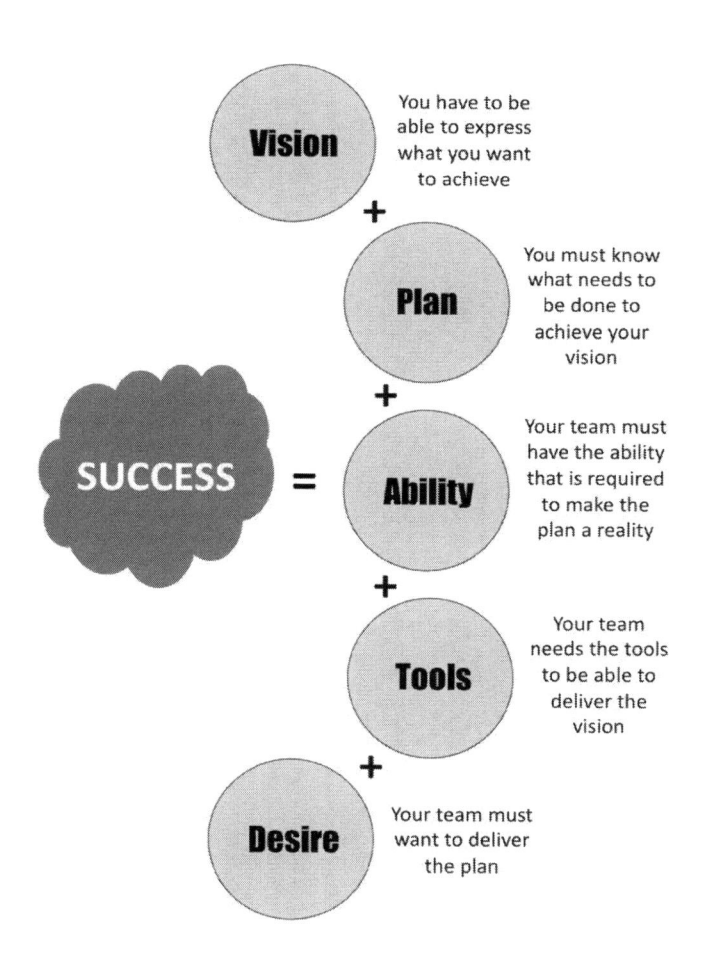

SUCCESS =

Vision + — You have to be able to express what you want to achieve

Plan + — You must know what needs to be done to achieve your vision

Ability + — Your team must have the ability that is required to make the plan a reality

Tools + — Your team needs the tools to be able to deliver the vision

Desire — Your team must want to deliver the plan

- Without a vision, there will be no change process.
- Without a plan, you could drift aimlessly, with individuals making lots of effort but all in the wrong place.
- Without the ability to meet any new requirements, your team will become frustrated and you will not progress.
- Without the tools to deliver the change, even the most resourceful of teams will struggle to succeed.
- Without the desire to make things happen, you will get resistance.

It's important to bear in mind that just because you or a group of people might be comfortable with change, some people find the very notion of re-doing or re-learning all they know very daunting. They can even go so far as to sabotage certain things to prove that the changes won't work.

It's the usual reaction to side-line these people or to ignore them. In fact, the right approach is to embrace them and spend time to understand what it is they fear and what you can do to help them become more comfortable.

Of course, there are some people who are happy with change only if it's their idea in the first place. These people must also be embraced, no matter how challenging or vocal they become.

COOKING FOR BUSINESS

Ingredients for effectively leading and managing change:

- Keep relevant parties informed
- Identify and tackle the barriers to change
- Have a clear vision of what success looks like
- Review progress regularly
- Make sure that everyone knows what is expected of them
- Ensure that the reasons for change are explained
- Encourage everyone to come up with new ideas
- Be open to change
- Ensure that change part of our everyday language
- Define the key steps for success
- Make contingency plans
- Understand the impact of change on your business
- Understand the impact of change on your customers
- Keep all parties informed of changes that will affect them
- Involve your customers in change initiatives
- Explore how to overcome the barriers to change
- Encourage constructive dissatisfaction
- Empower individuals to make necessary changes
- Encourage people to want to make a difference

- Maintain a positive attitude to change
- Learn from previous change initiatives
- Avoid 'quick fix' options
- Do what is right and not what is easy
- Detail precisely what the key benefits of change are
- Do not have a fear of failure
- Encourage everyone to get involved in change
- Balance short-term wins with long-term benefits
- Encourage individuals to find quick wins
- Ensure ownership for change across all team members
- Encourage new thinking across the whole business
- Celebrate success at every opportunity
- Embrace anyone who is uncomfortable with change
- Build a track record of ongoing change
- Build a dynamic business environment
- Create a dynamic culture
- Know how to make things happen
- Don't be afraid of change
- Embrace anyone that challenges the need for change
- Learn from past change experiences
- Encourage and reward change champions across the business
- Encourage constructive dissatisfaction
- Hold regular change seminars
- Look for examples of successful change initiatives

- Demonstrate that there is no such thing as 'a bad idea'
- Encourage open, healthy debate
- Treat people as individuals
- Maintain a fast pace across the business
- Explain that standing still is failure
- Encourage your managers to lead by example
- Encourage prudent risk-taking
- Learn from your mistakes and failures
- Build a team of people that are comfortable with change
- Ensure that senior managers lead by example
- Have a mechanism for regular 'change' updates
- Discourage complacency
- Invest in people as well as systems and products
- Embrace change with our customers
- Embrace change with our suppliers
- Have a clearly defined change process
- Collect and explore new ideas on a regular basis
- Support your people in going the 'extra mile'

"If you always do what you've always done, you'll always get what you've always got."
- Ed Foreman

THE SUPER SUPPORT TEAM

In most commercial organisations, the Support Team is the backbone of the business. It's all too easy to see them as the 'blunt end' of the business, but when Sales have secured distribution and Marketing have developed the mechanics to drive sales out, it's the Support Team that forms the vital link between your business, your customers and your consumers. Their role is critical to make things happen and ensure a successful outcome.

They need to have specific skills and they need to understand what the company is trying to achieve and what the individual customer plans are so that they can help deliver against the key actions that have been agreed.

They need to have a detailed product knowledge to enable them to effectively deal with any consumer feedback. Digitally, you can provide all the information that the customers and the consumers need but on a one-on-one telephone call, they can really convey the passion for the products and the interest that they have in delivering great service and a great product experience.

It's not the Sales or Marketing teams that process the incoming orders or book in the delivery slots, the Support Team do. It's not the Sales or Marketing teams that handle the consumer feedback. It's critical that the Support Team understand the importance of achieving deadlines and the impact of missing them. It's critical that they have the right information and tools at their disposal and they need ongoing support from all departments. Effective communication is vital if they're going to have any chance of fulfilling their commitments and responsibilities.

They should not only know their customer counterparts but should be able to meet with them on a regular basis to further cement the relationship and break down any potential barriers. If there was one team where relationships with the customers count for everything, this is it!

There will be product information to learn, systems and procedures to understand and technical and legal requirements to be aware of. Their role is multi-dimensional, but they're often not as highly regarded as they should be.

Think about your internal Support Team – they're the people who face your suppliers, customers and consumers. Invest in training and development for the team. Make sure that they have the knowledge and the skills to meet the constantly changing requirements and expectations of everyone that they come into contact with.

They need to be on top of their game all day, every day. Small investments in this team, bring massive benefits across the whole business. Start the process of making them an even more effective part of your team!

Ingredients for the super support team:

- Team members have friendly, outgoing personalities
- The whole team is results orientated

- Understands the service that we provide
- Strives to meets commitments
- Understands and focuses on priorities
- Works to a defined process
- Prepares thoroughly at the start of every day
- Displays lots of energy
- Individual members have strong interpersonal skills
- Tailor the approach to each individual customer
- Team members have strong influencing skills
- Understands how to handle numbers
- Is enthusiastic
- Demonstrates initiative
- Is self-motivating
- Understands the difference between features and benefits
- Checks the customers understanding of key facts
- Follows up on all commitments made to customers
- Ensures that the customer sees the benefits of the service
- Encourages the personal development of each team member
- Is effective at securing commitments
- Plans ahead
- Is well organised
- Meets regularly with the commercial teams
- Keeps up to date records
- Manages their time effectively
- Researches potential customers and suppliers
- Works well as part of the bigger team

COOKING FOR BUSINESS

- Makes considered, commercial decisions
- Understands the customer's business
- Communicates effectively at all levels
- Keeps a detailed diary of activities
- Solves problems
- Knows when to keep going and when to back down
- Knows the strengths and weaknesses of the service/product
- Understands the overall company objectives
- Demonstrates empathy
- Is motivated by success
- Reads trade-related press
- Has a sense of humour
- Shares information
- Strives for excellence
- Is ambitious and competitive
- Has a broad commercial outlook
- Questions effectively
- Knows how to handle objections
- Practices listening more than talking
- Has well-developed customer relationships
- Has well-developed IT skills
- Demonstrates common sense
- Challenges the status quo
- Gains something from every contact with the customer
- Stays up to date with all admin
- Generates new sales leads effectively
- Attends key customer/supplier meetings
- Plans effectively
- Knows where new business will come from
- Reviews progress regularly

- Adopts a sales-driven approach
- Celebrates success
- Finds constructive solutions to problems
- Understands how to add value to the customer relationship

THE GREAT LEADER

Ask people to name who they consider to be great leaders and the same names will come up every time – Richard Branson, Winston Churchill, Mary Barra, Nelson Mandela, etc.

When we look at these people, we can all appreciate how they led their respective teams but what can we learn from them? Were they born to do this, or did they learn the skills and acquire the knowledge to do so? Many people will look at these individuals and think that there's no way that they could do what these individuals did and yes, I agree that most of us won't get to lead an England football team or oversee the transition of our homeland, but we can all make a significant contribution to the workplace (and social environment) by understanding what makes a good leader into a great leader and changes a person from being a manager to being a true leader.

They are prepared to set the pace of the organisation, to lead from the front, and they energise others through their passion and commitment. They will not tolerate poor performance based on a person's attitude but will support individuals to increase performance, making time and resources available for development through coaching, mentoring and training.

They know that they're not always right and they know that they're not expected to know everything. They surround themselves with strong people and rely on those individuals to complement their own strengths and to supplement the areas where they are not so strong.

They're demanding but fair, focused but flexible. They play to their strengths and the strengths of others. They respect their people, they treat them fairly. They act with integrity at all times. They earn respect, they don't demand it.

They'll tell it as it is when needed and will not hesitate to have challenging conversations. They will go out of their way to help those individuals that go out of their way to get things done.

Even though they are the leader, they do not stop their quest, their hunger for learning. They constantly challenge themselves to learn as much as they can, to help more people in the future than they have in the past. They set an example which through their actions (not words), compels others to follow.

They are the type of individual who, if they read a book like this and find something that challenges them, they will do something about it.

> "Leadership and learning are indispensable to each other."
> - John F Kennedy

Ingredients for a great leader:

- Is articulate
- Is assertive
- Demonstrates confidence with numbers
- Has initiative
- Is honest and trustworthy
- Has strong interpersonal skills
- Has common sense
- Is well organised
- Makes things happen
- Is singled minded
- Is results orientated
- Acts decisively under pressure
- Approaches tasks with enthusiasm and passion
- Communicates effectively at all levels
- Manages time effectively
- Has empathy
- Is a team player
- Has a clear vision

COOKING FOR BUSINESS

- Is proactive
- Has humility
- Keeps people engaged
- Knows how to get things done
- Stays focused on the agreed plans
- Tells it as it is
- Is prepared to have difficult conversations
- Balances the needs of the business with the needs of the team
- Builds trust and rapport easily
- Knows how to energise a group
- Thinks strategically
- Is tenacious
- Makes time for himself/herself
- Leads by example
- Is prepared to take risks
- Makes time for other people
- Tackles challenges head-on
- Encourages diversity
- Is open to change
- Believes in his/her team
- Acts with consistency
- Treats everyone fairly
- Is self-aware
- Keeps promises
- Sets KPIs in conjunction senior managers
- Encourages honest feedback
- Lives in the 'real world'
- Understands the competitive environment
- Invests time to develop people
- Listens more than talks
- Has interests outside of work

- Is technologically and digitally 'savvy'
- Has common sense
- Challenges the way that things are done
- Puts the success of the team before his/her own success
- Makes time to spend with team members
- Communicates effectively at all levels
- Plans effectively
- Has the courage of his/her convictions
- Reviews progress regularly
- Keeps up to date with market information
- Understands the impact of external factors
- Finds constructive solutions to problems
- Is prepared to admit mistakes

THE EXCEPTIONAL MANAGER

We've all worked for at least one great manager in our careers. The one that invested in you, made you feel valued and helped you to make things happen. Likewise, I'm sure we've all worked for a manager that made us feel exactly the opposite – undervalued and unsupported.

So, with all our knowledge of what made the great manager great and what the other managers did that was not so great, it's easy to replicate those behaviours and actions which create a positive working environment where we get things done but we also feel good about doing those things.

The potential list of ingredients is extensive but based on your specific requirements, it's easy to reduce this list down to the core ingredients that once established and developed, will produce the type of managers that you need for long-term success.

We need to make sure that they have the right knowledge, the right skills and the right behaviours to ensure success. Those things that are essential and fit within the culture and direction of the business. Knowledge and skills are straightforward to identify and to assess. Behaviours can be more difficult to define but it's critical to have the right approach as nothing makes sense without it and you won't get the best out of the knowledge and skills that your people possess.

Managers need to possess the ability to communicate clearly and openly with their teams. To be able to give and to receive feedback on an ongoing basis. They need to clearly define role and responsibilities and to have a balanced approach – focused on getting the job done but also focused on engaging and motivating the people.

Ingredients for an exceptional manager:

- Is articulate
- Is assertive
- Is confident with numbers
- Has initiative
- Is honest and trustworthy
- Has strong interpersonal skills
- Has common sense
- Is well organised

- Is self-motivating
- Is motivated by success
- Is results orientated
- Acts decisively under pressure
- Approaches tasks enthusiastically
- Communicates effectively at all levels
- Manages time effectively
- Has empathy
- Is a team player
- Completes tasks that support the overall company vision
- Has a practical understanding of the individual team roles
- Knows what motivates individual team members
- Knows strengths and weaknesses of individual team members
- Sticks to agreed plans
- Is direct and to the point
- Is prepared to have difficult conversations
- Balances the needs of the business with the needs of the team
- Commands attention when presenting
- Builds trust and rapport easily
- Knows how to motivate the team
- Is trusted by the team
- Works consistently to get the job done
- Makes time for himself/herself
- Ensures detailed plans are in place for all key customers
- Knows how to influence internal and external customers
- Clarifies objectives

COOKING FOR BUSINESS

- Appraises team members' performance regularly
- Determines priorities
- Is open to change
- Meets deadlines consistently
- Challenges under performance
- Balances time between internal and external priorities
- Believes in his/herself
- Is respected by colleagues
- Sets KPIs with team members and peer group departments
- Able to give and willing to receive honest feedback
- Monitors KPIs regularly
- Understands the competitive environment
- Invests time to develop people
- Listens more than talks
- Has interests outside of work
- Has well developed IT skills
- Has common sense
- Challenges the status quo
- Communicates the successes of the team effectively
- Stays up to date with all admin
- Makes time to spend with team members
- Communicates well with other departments
- Plans effectively
- Has the courage of his/her own convictions
- Reviews progress regularly
- Keeps up to date with market information
- Understands the impact of external factors
- Finds constructive solutions to problems

RUNNING EFFECTIVE MEETINGS

Nothing has the potential to waste more time than a meeting. We've all been in meetings where people arrive late or are ill prepared and all that does is waste the time of every other person in the room. It's frustrating and it's disrespectful – not to mention wasteful when you consider the value of the salaries of the people sitting in the meeting room!

Meetings should be constructive and can achieve great things. Bringing people together to discuss, challenge and resolve complex situations is a great use of time but meetings that always take place on a certain day, at a set time, with the same attendees and in the same place, are not necessarily the best use of time for anyone.

All that's needed are simple changes and the support and commitment from everyone involved.

For example, the best way to start meetings on time is to do simply that, to start on time. Even if you're waiting for one or two people, start the meeting at the time stated. Once the regular offenders (and it is usually the same people) realise that people aren't going to wait, they'll adjust their behaviour and get there on time.

If you don't believe or realise the impact that starting a meeting let can have on your business, do this simple exercise:

1. Identify the number of people missing at the start of the meeting and note the amount of time that the start of the meeting is delayed by.

COOKING FOR BUSINESS

2. Look at the people in the meeting room waiting and based on their salaries, work out roughly home much money has been wasted by them having to wait.
3. Based on how often this happens, work out how much the 'wastage' is over the whole working year.

When I did this exercise recently, I was shocked to work out that we were wasting the equivalent of one whole person per year! In a small business that's a staggering amount to waste. Of course, there will always be the occasion when something out of the ordinary happens and people are delayed but it's often the same people who are late and it demonstrates a lack of respect or planning (you decide) and needs to be sorted out.

If you can't do a simple thing like start on time, then you have to ask some serious questions of your team and your business.

Also, don't be distracted by unplanned topics being brought into the conversation. Don't ignore them totally as they could be important in their own right but rather than letting them derail the whole meeting, use a 'parking lot' to leave the issues in a place that you can return to – either later in the meeting or on a future date.

It can be useful to have an agreed set of rules – a meeting 'etiquette' that is discussed, agreed and displayed around the office the keep people focused and on track.

Here's an example of a 'Meeting Etiquette' for reference but I would encourage you to see the list of ingredients to develop your own and start to get more out your meetings and waste less time!

Meeting Etiquette

1. All meetings will start on time – if you're not in the room at the agreed start time, the meeting will start without you
2. No mobile phones to be placed on the meeting table and all phones must be on silent
3. The agenda will be circulated 24 hours beforehand to allow for preparation
4. Minutes and agreed actions will be circulated within 24 hours of the end of the meeting
5. Meetings must not be scheduled to run 'back to back'
6. All attendees will be expected to participate
7. No AOB on any agenda
8. We will use the 'Parking Lot' to capture unplanned items and reschedule
9. All meetings will have the correct attendees
10. All meeting will end at the scheduled time – if we need more time, we will reschedule

Ingredients for effective meetings:

- Have a clear agenda
- Circulate the agenda before the meeting
- Have set time limits
- Have the right attendees
- Keeps to the agenda
- Have an assigned chairperson
- Choose the right environment
- Stay focused on the meeting objectives
- Avoid distractions
- Have a 'parking lot' to store unplanned items
- Ensure all attendees prepare thoroughly
- Have the right information and documents to hand
- Confirm meeting objectives at the start of the meeting
- Ensure all attendees make a contribution
- Ensure that people take notes where required
- Control discussion
- Encourage full participation
- Ensure that decisions are reached
- Create an environment where challenge is OK
- Allow time for questions
- Encourage free thinking
- Keep the time taken to a minimum
- Avoid back-to-back meetings
- Start on time
- End on time
- Do not allow AOB to be on the agenda
- Avoid 'follow on' meetings

- Ensure that attendees are prepared to listen
- Do not allow mobile phones on the meeting table
- Send out notes and action points promptly
- Complete agreed actions on time.

THE SUPER SALESPERSON

It was a long-held view that, if you wanted to be good in a sales career, you had to have the 'gift of the gab' – the ability to talk without fear or delay in public or in private. To talk at people rather than listen to them. Of course, it's true that it was traditional for a salesperson to have a huge range of products and the easiest way to present them was to simply talk at the customer.

As products have become more sophisticated and customers have become more demanding, thankfully the expectations of a salesperson have increased dramatically.

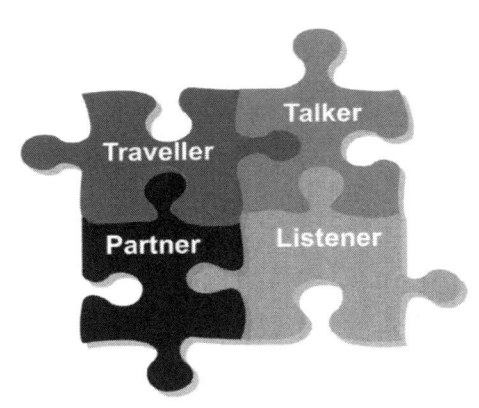

COOKING FOR BUSINESS

In the past, salespeople were often referred to as 'Travellers' and basically all they were there to do was to build a relationship with the customer so that if and when they needed an order, they would call them. As time went by and more and more products became available, it was necessary for the salesperson to present their larger range of products but as time was limited, they were forced to simply talk at the customer, relaying endless facts and figures in order to persuade the customer to give them an order.

It became apparent over time that this approach – the 'hard sell' – was becoming increasingly ineffective and the salesperson had to learn new skills and be able question the customer and to listen to what the customer wanted or needed. To be able to question effectively remains of paramount importance.

As the salesperson learned more about the customer and became skilled at matching products and services to meet specific requirements, they became trusted by their customers and were seen as a partner in whom they could confide and who would be able to work them to develop their business.

Long gone are the days where the salesperson was referred to, often derogatively, as a 'rep'. They now need to be a blend of salesperson, account manager, advisor, product expert and pragmatic business partner.

They need to have passion for the business and for the products. They need to have comprehensive product, industry and customer knowledge and be able to use that knowledge in a way that presents a sound business case for why the customer should or should not buy.

They need to have a broad network of contacts to be able to get things done and they must have an eye for detail and the list of expected actions is long and very comprehensive.

To be a great salesperson doesn't mean that you need to do superhuman or extraordinary things. You simply need to do ordinary things exceptionally and consistently well.

> "How you sell matters. What your process is matters. But how your customers feel when they engage with you matters more."
> - Tiffani Bova

Ingredients for the super salesperson:

- Is results orientated
- Has a friendly, outgoing personality
- Is a good negotiator
- Is resilient
- Has established networks within key customers
- Always meets deadlines
- Understands and focuses on prioritising
- Works to a defined structure
- Prepares thoroughly before every call
- Has a proven track record
- Has lots of energy
- Has strong interpersonal skills
- Is honest and trustworthy
- Has strong influencing skills
- Understands how to handle numbers
- Is enthusiastic
- Has initiative
- Is self-motivating
- Is an effective leader
- Understands the difference between features and benefits
- Checks customers' understanding
- Follows up on all commitments made to customers
- Always ensures the customer sees the benefits of the service
- Knows how and when to use 'open' and 'closed' questions
- Closes effectively
- Plans ahead

- Is well organised
- Communicates effectively at all levels
- Keeps up to date records of competitors services/products
- Manages time effectively
- Works well in a team
- Makes considered decisions
- Uses the strengths of other team members
- Understands the customer's business
- Is articulate
- Keeps a detailed diary of activities
- Is good at solving problems
- Knows when to back down
- Knows strengths and weaknesses of the service/product
- Has mutually agreed business plans in place with key customers
- Shows empathy
- Is motivated by success
- Is assertive
- Is confident
- Is ambitious and competitive
- Has a broad commercial understanding
- Asks lots of questions
- Knows how to overcome objections
- Is adaptable
- Has common sense
- Challenges the status quo
- Gains something from every customer visit
- Is willing to accept new ideas
- Plans effectively
- Knows where new business will come from
- Sets clear objectives and measures and

monitors progress
- Is self-aware
- Understands the market
- Finds constructive solutions to problems
- Has a disciplined approach to work
- Knows what to focus on
- Has a sense of humour

THE GREAT SALES CALL

We all strive for the perfect sales call; the one where we get what we want and the customer feels good about it. But, not only do you need to ask yourself what you need to do to make a great sales call, you also need to identify how you can replicate it time after time.

The answer is actually quite simple and it's all about having the right ingredients, bound together in a straightforward structure that is consistently used.

A typical structure would be:

1. Preparation
2. Introduction
3. Questioning
4. Presentation
5. Close
6. Overcome objections

7. Review
8. Follow-up

This structure or 'Steps of the Call' as it's often referred to, is the backbone of any consistent performance. You can tailor the structure to meet your own specific needs and your teams can use it time after time to achieve outstanding, consistent results. Above all, any call structure should be simple and straightforward.

The 'Steps of the Call'

- **Preparation**

    Sell thro

    Performance to date – where am I against my plan?

    Promotional effectiveness

    Digital activity

    Store visit – instore presence

    Web check – online presence

    Availability

    Opportunities

    Objectives

    Follow-up from last call

    Customer objectives

Customer business performance

- **Questioning**

    Establishing the current situation

    Understanding what might have changed

    What's working for them?

    What activity are they investing in?

    What are your competitors up to?

- **Presentation**

    Tell a story

    What's happening?

    What's the impact?

    What's my proposal/idea?

    How will it work?

    What's in it for them?

- **Closing**

    How will you ask for the order?

- **Overcoming objections**

    Sidestep initial objections

    Find the true objection

- **Review**

    How did I do?

    Did I question?

    Did I listen?

    Did I demonstrate empathy?

Did I achieve what I set out to?

Identify things to work on for the next meeting

- **Follow up**

    Email to customer confirming actions

    Internal Contact Report to confirm actions

- **Next meeting**

    What needs to be on the agenda?

Ingredients for a great sales call:

- Has a defined process
- Has a clear objective
- Is well prepped
- Follows on from a previous call
- Builds the relationship with key contacts
- Extends the relationship across the business
- Adds to your understanding of the customer
- Is well researched
- Incorporates 'live', up-to-date information
- Uses available technology
- Solves problems
- Deals with objections
- Allows for open discussion
- Addresses customer concerns
- Answers customer queries
- Involves a broad range of people
- Allows time for questions
- Forms part of the broader customer business

plan
- Has no surprises
- Delivers results for both parties
- Clarifies and explains
- Is not rushed
- Does not 'drag on'
- Motivates the customer
- Allows time to explore new ideas
- Balances the needs of the customer with the needs of the seller
- Recognises and incorporates key information
- Can be repeated each time
- Builds understanding
- Achieves results
- Sets the scene for the next call

MAKING MORE OF YOUR TIME

How do you get the most out of your day – for business and for personal reward?

Knowing what's important is the key to managing your time more effectively. What's important from a business point of view and what's important from a personal point of view. There is no predetermined right or wrong when it comes to a 'work-life' balance. It is entirely up to you. What suits one person will not necessarily suit another. If I choose to work at weekends, it's my choice and just because I choose to work, I don't expect others to do so.

Being absolutely crystal clear on what's important is crucial and the ability to recognise the difference between 'important' and 'urgent' is fundamental to getting more done in the same amount of time. If something's important, it's always important. Just because something is urgent does not mean that it is necessarily important. It may well have been poorly planned by someone else and by the time you get to hear about it, the deadline's looming and it is urgent.

It's what you achieve and get done that makes you effective, not the number of things that you commit to. Being busy is not being effective. Managing tasks in a logical, efficient, thoughtful way is what will increase your effectiveness.

Discipline yourself: be on time for meetings and don't waste other people's time by being poorly organised. Prepare thoroughly for every meeting (internal and external) and be aware of all times of how you're progressing against your KPIs.

Manage your tasks more effectively and gain more time and energy for things outside work – family, hobbies, health, sport, holidays.

> "A man who dares waste one hour of time has not discovered the value of life."
> - Charles Darwin

COOKING FOR BUSINESS

If you want to see a truly practical demonstration of how to get more into a day if you try a different approach, check out my 496 Kitchen channel on YouTube.

With a simple rearranging of your diary, by breaking the big task down into smaller parts and by scheduling them at the start of the day, it's incredible how much more you can get out of a day – and still have time for life outside of work!

Ingredients for making the most of your time:

- Understand your priorities
- Share priorities with team members
- Build in time for yourself
- Schedule key tasks when you have most energy
- Incorporate your 'To Do' list into your diary
- Challenge the need for recurring meetings
- Start meetings on time
- Work on the priorities first
- Avoid distractions
- Do not arrange back-to-back meetings
- Be disciplined with your time
- Do not waste other people's time
- Be prepared for all meetings
- Start on time
- Leave on time
- Build flexibility into your diary
- Build the everyday activities around your priorities

- Do not allow other people to put things in your diary
- Take regular breaks
- Manage your own diary before you manage other people's
- Consider the impact of your actions on other people
- Set deadlines based on priority, not rank
- Allocate time to spend on the things that you enjoy
- Deliver on all commitments made
- Manage distractions
- Delegate repeating tasks
- Eliminate re-work
- Break key tasks into smaller parts
- Get used to saying 'No'
- Build in planning time
- Don't let 'perfect' be the enemy of 'good'

THE GREAT PRESENTER

The skill of an effective presenter is in being able to convey a message or a concept in a clear, logical and engaging way. They link points together to help understanding and to take the audience on a journey to the destination that they want.

For a long time, the simple steps of – **Tell them what you're going to tell them** – **Tell them** – **Tell them what you've told them** – were more than enough of a structure to be able to deliver a presentation that made sense to the audience, allowed them to assimilate the key facts and to understand what was the expected of them. In fact, those three steps still are the basis of every great presentation, but with the amount of technology at everyone's disposal, audience expectations have increased and the opportunities to create a truly memorable and effective presentation have increased dramatically.

Of course, you can speak 'off the cuff' and without preparation, but very few people can actually do this with any degree of professionalism, control and impact. Preparation is the key to a great presentation and by preparation, I do not mean taking time to think about all the fancy tricks that you're going to incorporate. You must make time to think about the tone, the pace, the content and of course, the supporting materials.

Always remember that the more slides you have does not mean that your presentation will be better. Far from it. It really is a case of 'less is more' and you should focus on how you convey the message with emotion rather than relying on the slides to do it for you. If a great presentation was only dependent on the slides that you included, there would be no need to ever make a presentation. We could simply send the slides to each member of the audience and expect them to understand exactly what we were trying to say!

Great presenters don't rush their preparation and they review a number of times to see what they can leave out to focus on the main messages even more. Less content generally means more impact overall – as long as you treat that content in the right way. They rehearse to gauge the appropriate speed and overall timing and to achieve the correct tone and posture to make sure that each key point is understood by the audience.

They involve the audience though eye contact and targeted questions – some rhetorical, some actual questions. All the time they're controlling the audience's emotions. Using different speeds of speech and different tones and gestures to add interest and aid recall. They manage the environment that they're in. They get to a venue early and check out the dynamics. Nothing is left to chance. They know that thorough preparation pays off every time.

We all love to listen to a great presentation and there's every reason why with attention in a few key areas, you can nail it every time. Not everyone has the natural confidence to stand up and present to a group of strangers or as some people find even worse, a group of friends or colleagues. Confidence will come from the fact that you have prepared thoroughly, rehearsed sufficiently and you know your subject. If you're lacking in any one of these areas, then you deserve to be nervous and although you might get lucky, it's doubtful that your presentation will have the impact that you wanted it to.

"Make sure you have finished speaking before your audience has finished listening."
- Dorothy Sarnoff

Ingredients for a great presenter:

- Have a clear message
- Be brief and to the point
- Use jargon sparingly
- Limit the number of slides
- Use PowerPoint and props as support only
- Tell a story
- Use emotion as well as reason
- Maintain an open, confident posture
- Rehearse before each presentation
- Learn how to handle interruptions with confidence
- Present at a comfortable pace
- Speak with clarity
- Use straightforward language to boost understanding
- Keep slides uncluttered
- Be yourself
- Use humour appropriately
- Never read from the screen
- Vary the tone of your voice to create and maintain interest
- Allow time for questions
- Work to a defined structure or process
- Be aware of the audience's body language
- Control your movement
- Maintain eye contact
- Tailor the message to every different audience
- Invest time to find the right words
- Identify what to leave out to create greater impact

- Work actively to engage the audience
- Speak with passion
- Use pauses to heighten interest
- Summarise effectively
- Stand to 'present' and sit down to 'discuss'

THE WIN-WIN NEGOTIATION

The best negotiators aren't the people who have the most experience, they're not the tallest people and certainly don't have to be the most qualified people. All successful negotiators have one thing in common – they prepare thoroughly for every negotiation situation.

The most effective negotiators control their emotions so that they can remain alert and objective. They do not let themselves get boxed into corners and they certainly do not let themselves be pressured by artificial time deadlines. Time pressure in any negotiation is never good for all participants and will always favour one of the parties more than the others. Be wary of such a tactic and be certain to challenge any deadlines that are set during the negotiation process.

They invest time to consider the position of the other party and to think about what a good deal would look like for them. They work hard to identify the concessions that they can ask for and they carefully cost all of their own 'tradeables' so that they know exactly how much they have given away so they can ensure they get at least the same, but preferably more, in return. It takes a bit of effort to pull all the information together but once you have it, you'll be much better equipped and you'll feel much more in control.

Use the planning document to work out not just what something costs you but also what the value is to the other party. Something may actually cost you very little but may be vital to the business that you're negotiating with. Use that perceived value to secure concessions that are worth far more to you.

Work out beforehand what concessions you can ask for and be sure to hang onto any concessions that you gain as you go through the process. You may secure an early agreement that looks less favourable to the other party as the negotiation develops. Remember, it's now yours to give back, it's not for the other party to take back and if you choose to surrender something that you've gained, you must get something extra in return.

Be sure to concede slowly – if your first concession represents a significant change to your original offer, you will raise the expectation that the next concession could be just as large. Make the other party work hard for any concession that you might give.

Above all, stay calm and focused and remember, you're looking for 'Win-Win'. There's no point in securing a deal at the expense of the future relationship.

One element that is often overlooked is the location or environment in which the negotiation is due to take place. I've experienced many negotiations that have taken place in the reception area of the company concerned. It's usually within earshot of other people and worse still, it could be your competitor that overhears what's being said. These open locations do not allow for full and frank conversations and they are often chosen as they allow for 'steam roller' tactics where the other party does not want a discussion, they just want you to agree to their demands. The location does affect the negotiation and if you feel uncomfortable, do whatever you can to move to a different area.

Being as prepared as you can be will give you an enormous boost of confidence and time invested in preparation will always bring benefits in any negotiation.

> "In business as in life, you don't get what you deserve, you get what you negotiate."
> - Chester L Karras

COOKING FOR BUSINESS

NEGOTIATION 'TRADE-ABLES'

Trade-Ables	Actual Cost	Value to Customer		
		Low	Medium	High

Ingredients for a win-win negotiation:

- Know the cost and value your 'tradeables'
- Have a clear negotiating position
- Be clear about what your desired outcome is
- Offer concessions slowly
- Think what's in it for the other party
- Identify concessions that you can ask for
- Think creatively
- Don't be rushed into making a decision
- Know your 'walk away' position
- Look for clues in other people's body language
- Work to a defined process
- Ask open questions
- Cost all concessions carefully
- Make sure the other party see the value in your proposal
- Don't be afraid to be first to reveal your expectations
- Understand which benefits to emphasise key
- Never give a concession without gaining something in return
- Make sure you 'bank' any concessions gained
- Understand what influence you can have in each negotiation
- Be realistic in your demands
- Make sure all concessions gained are tangible
- Maintain your flexibility throughout the process
- Avoid deadlock
- Establish the motivations of the other party early in the process

COOKING FOR BUSINESS

- Be firm with your demands
- Listen actively
- Be aware of your own body language
- Be prepared to call a 'time-out' if needed
- Control your emotions
- Think and act 'Win-Win'
- Be patient – it's not a race

Making Things Happen

DECIDING ON AN ACTION PLAN

Before you can decide and agree what needs to happen to get you where you want to be, you need to understand where you are now. This is really straightforward to do and each person should be asked to rate the current situation against each of the 'ingredients' on a scale of 1 to 10 – 1 being 'we're nowhere near' and 10 being 'we're already doing this or behaving in this way'.

Again, everyone will have an opinion so take time to listen and explore them. Discussion at this stage will lead to a smoother action plan in the long-term.

COOKING FOR BUSINESS

Once you've agreed where you are, set out the actions that need to happen and assign responsibilities. Agree milestones to review progress and maintain momentum.

Look out for signs of progress and be ready to give feedback at all times. Remember that feedback should be:

- **Honest**
  There's no benefit in not telling it like it is.
- Timely
  If you see something, don't wait to give feedback – especially positive feedback!
- **Two-way**
  Listen to what people have to say as well as giving opinions.
- **Appropriate**
  Keep things in context and make the level and tone of feedback fit the level of achievement.
- **Balanced**
  There will be a need for **Corrective** feedback (putting things right) and **Constructive** feedback (reinforcing the positive feelings within the group).

Give people space to breathe and allow them to get on with things. Maintain a safe distance and don't overmanage the situation. You'll just end up stifling their enthusiasm and their performance. Be available to give support and to praise where appropriate and stay close enough to step in to help where necessary.

The Performance Improvement Grid

One really effective way of setting out an action plan, one that can be personalised to each team and for every individual, is to use a simple grid – The Performance Improvement Grid (PIG).

You'll see that the grid is divided into four quadrants that allow you to detail specific actions that recognise the positives and the development areas alongside each other and allow a 'balanced approach' that's easy to monitor and review on an ongoing basis.

When using the PIG to give feedback or review progress, it's best if you work through the sheet from top left quadrant (Start Doing), finishing on the bottom right quadrant (Do More). This way, you give yourself the chance to end on a positive note, recognising what's gone well and giving encouragement.

COOKING FOR BUSINESS

Figure 1 - PIG – Performance Improvement Grid

Start Doing	Stop Doing
Do Differently	Do More

Start Doing

The first quadrant is for you to identify those actions that don't currently happen, or the individual doesn't currently do but are required if you are to achieve your desired result. You can make these as simple and straightforward as you like and in doing so, you'll not only make it easy for the individual to take the first step, but you'll also create opportunities to give feedback which is essential if you're going to maintain momentum and focus.

Stop Doing

The next quadrant is for you to identify those actions or behaviours that are no longer required as you head towards your end goal. On the face of it, this could seem quite a negative angle to take but in reality there could be tasks in there that are currently part of everyday working life (such as reporting on key areas) that you may be reviewing or stopping as part of your new ways of doing things, In this instance, it's a very positive discussion and actually 'cements' the idea that this is actually happening.

Do Differently

In this section, you can capture those tasks or actions that already take place but in the light of what you're trying to achieve, need to be done in a different way. For example, a verbal update instead of a written report or a telephone call instead of a regular face-to-face meeting. As previously, the fact that we commit to do things differently and we are detailing and tracking those things, will provide reassurance and energy to the whole process.

Do More

The final quadrant is where you can identify positive events or behaviours that you need to see more of. In some cases, these are areas that are often seen as 'nice to do' rather than 'need to do'. Typically, in FMCG or Consumer Goods businesses, activities such as store visits are often pushed back as they're not seen as vital to the progress of the organisation. In reality, nothing could be further from the truth. How else will you know that what you think is happening is actually happening? Your interpretation of your day-to-day business results will be based on your belief of what's happening in store. Far better to check on this rather than make assumptions. You'll also see all the other things that influence your sales – competitor activity, amount of space, location in store, pricing – to name just a few.

Use the PIG as the basis for all ongoing review and feedback, and for those actions where you need a defined date for completion, you may find it useful to add a column for the date that the specific task needs to be completed by or by setting and committing to regular review dates, you can keep track from week to week as you progress.

Follow-up

Now that you've completed the session, you have your list of ten to twelve ingredients that will form the 'backbone' of your transition from where you are to where you want to be. The momentum that you've created is fantastic and you now need to act to put a number of things in place to maintain this momentum and to make sure all participants progress in the way that you want them to and at the time you want them to.

A further dimension to this process is that you will have started to realise that the levels of knowledge and skill required and also the behaviours expected to be able to deliver your vision of success will have to be reviewed. Don't let this alarm you or put you off from even starting the process as you'll probably have access to the knowledge that you need and the skill that you need to develop already existing within your business. Take time to work with the managers to assess where individuals are in respect of their strengths and development areas and use the strengths that you have in house to develop that knowledge or skills in others. In this way, you'll make best use of the resources you have and you'll motivate those people involved which will in turn increase their overall level of contribution.

This assessment of individual strengths and development areas will also help you to start building a succession plan – harnessing the talent you have and building on it for the future good of the business overall. Be careful not to promise a promotion or a future position but do make it clear what you and the individual team members could be working towards.

Of course, if there is a serious skills or knowledge gap, you may have to consider the use of a third party to assist you in these specific areas. Explore your own network and you'll probably find that you have the contacts already to be able to do this is a timely and cost-effective way.

> "People will always do what you inspect, not what you expect."
> - Anonymous

Setting reviews

Make reviews regular but short occurrences. Get people used to sharing their progress, their successes and also any delays and potential failures that they may have experienced. Use the energy across the group to solve the challenges that you face and use the reviews to allow you to celebrate success. Not everything you try will work first time and it's really important to establish whether it was a 'miss' or a 'mistake'. Was it the right thing to do or try and we've just been unfortunate, and we've faced challenges that we couldn't foresee? Or was it actually the wrong thing to do? Take time to reflect honestly and objectively; you won't get everything right and don't beat yourself up unnecessarily.

Appraising performance

As well as reviewing the completion or otherwise of key tasks, make time to review the individual performances that support those achievements. Are individuals struggling because of their own level of knowledge and skills? Are they continuing to approach those tasks in the right frame of mind? There are a number of factors that can affect individual performance and you need to direct, support or coach as appropriate. Certainly, if they appear to be struggling, you should not leave them to continue alone and without any support at all. Sometimes all it takes is a simple word of encouragement to get them back 'in the groove' and performing at the level that's needed.

Celebrating success

Be sure to grab every opportunity to celebrate individual and team successes as they happen. The feel-good factor associated with being appreciated by your peer group and senior management is not to be underestimated. No matter how small the achievement is, simple and timely recognition will increase confidence and overall performance. From a simple 'thank you' in an email to an evening at the pub with the team 'toasting' each other's success, make sure that you take time not only to recognise individual achievement and success, but also that you find ways to celebrate those achievements and successes.

Summary

As I said at the start of the book, what I wanted to provide was a reference point to use either on its own or in conjunction with things that you're already doing. I wanted to challenge you to consider not only getting the best 'ingredients' into your business but also to help you to treat them in the right way to get the best results.

I hope that through the various steps that I've outlined, I've been able to show you that by following a simple process, you can achieve great things. How by harnessing the talent that you already have in your business you can 'upskill' all of your team and keep them engaged and motivated.

Approaching new challenges with an open mind and a positive outlook is essential but without a structured approach and a defined plan of action, all that positive energy won't deliver the results that you're looking for. Intent is one thing but taking action is everything.

Sometimes the scale of the task that you face can look daunting. The end result that you want seems so distant from where you are, you simply stay where you are and 'make do' with the current situation. However, if you break those goals into manageable tasks, they become much easier to achieve.

My goal was to fill this book with useful ideas and tools but also to make it compact enough to allow you to read it and understand the process in a limited period of time. For example, during a train journey or on a flight. These are times where being in a different environment can often help you to see things in a different way and can make you aware that there are other approaches that could bring different results.

The content and the process that I've described could in no way be described as extraordinary. Far from it. In fact, my intention was not only to make them ordinary and straightforward, but also to make them attainable. We can all do ordinary things. The trick is to learn to do them extraordinarily well.

"Be courageous or be complacent. Either way you'll get the results that you deserve."

ABOUT THE 496 PARTNERSHIP

The 496 Partnership was born out of my experience that properly motivated and engaged individuals can achieve great things. Too often, individual talent is underused and underdeveloped because of a lack of focus and support. My approach is one-on-one, 'partnering' with talented individuals and working with them to help them achieve their maximum potential. Very much 'just in time' rather than 'just in case'.

It's a partnership because not only do I get to work in a close and very focused way with individuals, but I also work with a team of experienced, practical and highly motivated business professionals who share my beliefs and goals. My passion is 'Making People Count'.

Why 496?

496 is a 'perfect number' – it's divisible by: 1, 2, 4, 8, 16, 31, 62, 124 and 248. If you take all of those individual component numbers and add them together, the total comes to 496. Just as the number 496 is made up of multiples of smaller numbers, organisations also consist of many different components – departments, teams and individuals. Indeed, our own lives have many different 'components' that shape who and what we are.

With any one of the numbers missing, any components missing or any members of the team not performing, we cannot get to 100%. Likewise, in our own lives we often hear the phrase, 'I'm not feeling 100%.' We know that it doesn't mean that everything is wrong. It simply means that one aspect of our day-to-day lives is causing us concern.

The 496 Kitchen on You Tube

Working with my digital partner, Lion Island Media, I have produced a series of short videos that support the topics that are contained in this book.

In each of the videos, I take a quick look at each subject and talk about the key ingredients required to make each 'recipe' a success. They're designed for busy people and allow for quick consumption and digestion!

Check them out and let me know what you think. I'd love to hear your feedback!

Want to bring this to life in your business?

If you feel energised and inspired by what you've read but feel that you'd like assistance to bring it to life within your business, why not get in touch and talk through how I can work with you and your team to run an individual session, tailored for you and your business?

This could be either an individual or a team session that will take you through the process from start to finish, ensuring that you get full buy-in and support at every stage and agreeing action plans to make sure that the necessary changes are made and embedded within your business.

Get in touch for a no-obligation discussion and let me know exactly what you're trying to achieve. I'd be delighted to discuss your specific requirements and where I can help you.

vance@496partnership.com

MAKING PEOPLE COUNT

About the author

Vance Withers was born in the county of Somerset in the United Kingdom and is an experienced, passionate commercial leader with over forty years of international sales and management experience.

His passion for developing people started early on in his career when he secured the position of National Sales Trainer and having established the procedures and systems for developing the sales team, he moved into his first team management role at the age of twenty-three. He quickly established a reputation for supporting and developing people, as well as achieving outstanding business results. He worked for a number of years as a management consultant, before returning to an International commercial role.

COOKING FOR BUSINESS

He started the 496 Partnership in 2017 to allow him to get back to his passion for helping individuals and businesses to achieve their full potential.

He is an accomplished musician and chef, a keen collector of antiques and an enthusiastic mountain biker and boater.

He currently lives in the village of Birtsmorton, Worcestershire, with his wife Karen.

PLEASE NOTE

In business as with any recipe, simply having the right ingredients available will not produce guaranteed results. How you treat the individual 'ingredients', how you determine your goals, how you monitor your progress, how you engage with your people and the individual actions that you personally take will significantly influence the results that you can achieve.

Printed in Great Britain
by Amazon